W9-BJQ-936

TO

LOVE

BABIES ARE SPECIAL™

A CELEBRATION OF A NEW ARRIVAL

COMPILED BY
LUCY MEAD

GRAMERCY BOOKS
NEW YORK

This 2002 edition is published by Gramercy Books™, an imprint of
Random House Value Publishing, Inc. 280 Park Avenue, New York, N.Y. 10017.

Gramercy Books™ and design are trademarks of Random House Value Publishing, Inc.

Random House
New York • Toronto • London • Sydney • Auckland
http://www.randomhouse.com/

Interior Design: Karen Ocker Design, New York
Printed and bound in Singapore

Library of Congress Cataloging-in-Publication Data

Babies are special / compiled by Lucy Mead.
    p. cm.
   ISBN 0-517-22062-8
    1. Infants--Quotations, maxims, etc. I. Mead, Lucy.

   PN6084.I48 B31702002
   305.232--dc21
                      2001057399

9 8 7 6 5 4 3 2 1

BABIES ARE SPECIAL™

Every child is born a genius.

R. BUCKMINSTER FULLER

Bye, baby bunting.
Daddy's gone a-hunting
Gone to get a rabbit skin
To wrap up baby bunting in.

OLD NURSERY RHYME

Being born is like being kidnapped. And then sold into slavery.

ANDY WARHOL

Pregnancy is the only time in a woman's
life she can help God work a miracle.

ERMA BOMBECK

A baby is God's opinion that the world should go on.
Never will a time come when the most marvelous recent
invention is as marvelous as a newborn child.

CARL SANDBURG

A child is a curly, dimpled lunatic.

RALPH WALDO EMERSON

In the eyes of its mother every beetle is a gazelle.

MOROCCAN PROVERB

A baby is an inestimable blessing and bother.

MARK TWAIN

He's my wonderful, precious little Buddha. He eats like a champion. He sleeps peacefully—and he's the apple of his daddy's eye.

SHARON STONE

I have no name.
I am but two days old.
What shall I call thee?
I happy am,
Joy is my name.
Sweet joy befall thee!

WILLIAM BLAKE in *Songs of Innocence*

...our children just don't come with guarantees, and maybe that's one of the things that makes them so breathtakingly special to us.

BETSY HART, CNN and Fox News Channel commentator

Babies and the old are permitted self-absorption.
In between, it provokes resentment.

MASON COOLEY, aphorist

The truth is, no matter how trying they become,
babies two and under don't have the ability to make
moral choices, so they can't be "bad." That category
only exists in the adult mind.

ANNE CASSIDY in *Working Mother*

All children, except one, grow up.

J.M. BARRIE, *Peter Pan*

Flowers are words which
even a baby can understand.

ARTHUR C. COXE

A person's a person no matter how small.

Dr. Seuss (Theodore Geisel)

If I had influence with the good fairy who is supposed to preside over the christening of all children, I should ask that her gift to each child in the world would be a sense of wonder so indestructible that it would last throughout life…

Rachel Carson, author of *The Silent Spring*

The sweetest flowers in all the world—a baby's hands.

Algernon Charles Swinburne

There's only one pretty child in the world, and every parent has it.

Proverb

If God had meant for us to be naked,
we would have been born that way.

MARK TWAIN

Baby's room …must have wallpaper with clowns holding
blue, red, and green balloons. Baby's room should be
close enough to your room so that you can hear baby cry,
unless you want to get some sleep, in which case baby's
room should be in Peru.

DAVE BARRY

Grandmothers are the people who take delight
in hearing babies breathing into the telephone.

ANONYMOUS

11

Sweet babe, in thy face
Soft desires I can trace,
Secret joys and secret smiles,
Little pretty infant wiles.

WILLIAM BLAKE, "A Cradle Song"

Truth, which is important to a scholar, has got to be concrete. And there is nothing more concrete than dealing with babies, burps and bottles, frogs and mud.

JEANE J. KIRKPATRICK, United Nations
ambassador, in *Newsweek*

Infancy conforms to nobody: all conform to it, so that one babe commonly makes four or five out of the adults who prattle and play to it.

RALPH WALDO EMERSON

Child, the current of your breath is six days long.
You lie, a small knuckle on my white bed;
lie, fisted like a snail, so small and strong
at my breast. Your lips are animals; you are fed
with love.

ANNE SEXTON, "Unknown Girl
in the Maternity Ward"

Loving a baby is a circular business, a kind of feedback loop. The more you give the more you get and the more you get the more you feel like giving.

PENELOPE LEACH

Children are a kind of confirmation of life. The only form of immortality that we can be sure of.

PETER USTINOV

Childbirth is more admirable than conquest, more amazing
than self-defense, and as courageous as either one.

GLORIA STEINEM

The old system of having a baby was much better than the
new system, the old system being characterized by the fact
that the man didn't have to watch.

DAVE BARRY

Think of stretch marks as pregnancy service stripes.

JOYCE ARMOR, WKRP, CINCINNATI

I think it is such a privilege to give a baby its first home
inside your body.

CELINE DION

There is no way out of the experience except through
it, because it is not really your experience at all but
the baby's. Your body is the child's instrument of birth.

PENELOPE LEACH

Whenever a woman gives birth to a child,
she remembers the hard work no more,
for the joy that a child has been born into the world.

JOHN 16:20

If men had to have babies
they would only ever have one each.

DIANA, Princess of Wales

Babies are always more trouble than you thought—and more wonderful.

The great high of winning Wimbledon lasts for about a week. You go down in the record book, but you don't have anything tangible to hold on to. But having a baby—there isn't any comparison.

CHRIS EVERT LLOYD

No baby shall at any time be quartered in a house where there are no soft laps, no laughter, or no love.

ERMA BOMBECK

Then, miracle of miracles, as I picked her up and held her close, she picked up her head and looked at me.

I know that I'm supposed to believe that newborn babies can't really pick up their heads and see…but no one could ever convince me, for I was holding a new life, a fresh chance, another promise that although lives we love end, lives we will love begin.

LOIS WYSE, *Grandchildren are so much fun,*
I should have had them first

We have these striking pictures of Dylan around eight months into Catherine's [Zeta-Jones] pregnancy, and he looks just like her. He has Catherine's mouth, nose and eyes. The thing we didn't see, which was incredible when he first came out, was this huge dimple on his chin. I thought, "Whew. I've got some family genes in there."

MICHAEL DOUGLAS

Whenever I held my newborn baby in my arms, I used
to think that what I said and did to him could have an
influence not only on him but on all whom he met, not
only for a day or a month or a year, but for all eternity—
a very challenging and exciting thought for a mother.

ROSE KENNEDY

Having a child is surely the most beautifully
irrational act that two people in love can commit.

BILL COSBY

In the sheltered simplicity of the first days after a baby
is born, one sees again the magical closed circle, the
miraculous sense of two people existing only for each
other, the tranquil sky reflected on the face of the
mother nursing her child.

ANNE MORROW LINDBERGH

With two sons born eighteen months apart, I operated mainly on automatic pilot through the ceaseless activity of their early childhood. I remember opening the refrigerator late one night and finding a roll of aluminum foil next to a pair of small red tennies. Certain that I was responsible for the refrigerated shoes, I quickly closed the door and ran upstairs to make sure I had put the babies in their cribs instead of the linen closet.

MARY KAY BLAKELY in *American Mom*

Babies don't need fathers, but mothers do. Someone who is taking care of a baby needs to be taken care of.

AMY HECKERLING, director of *Guess Who's Talking*

Children are the anchors
that hold a mother to life.

SOPHOCLES

A soiled baby, with a neglected nose, cannot
be conscientiously regarded as a thing of beauty.

MARK TWAIN

One of the most important things to remember about
infant care is: never change diapers in midstream.

DON MARQUIS

When Charlie first saw our child, our Mary, he said all
the proper things for a new father. He looked upon the
poor little red thing and blurted, "She's more beautiful
than the Brooklyn Bridge."

HELEN HAYES

Babies are bits of stardust,
Blown from the hand of God.
Lucky the woman who knows
The pangs of birth,
For she has held a star.

LARRY BARRETTO, author of *The Indiscreet Years*

I thought I had forgotten how to hold a
baby—but my arms remember.

Anonymous

My child looked at me and I looked back at him in the
delivery room, and I realized that out of a sea of infinite
possibilities it came down to this: a specific person, born
on the hottest day of the year, conceived on Christmas Eve,
made by his father and me miraculously from scratch.

ANNA QUINDLEN

The planning is under way, negotiations are taking place, and I'm willing to predict a successful conclusion.

BRAD PITT on having a baby

A new baby is like the beginning of all things: wonder, hope, a dream of possibilities. In a world that is cutting down its trees to build highways, babies are almost the only remaining link with nature…from which we spring.

EDA LeSHAN

I love to think that the day you're born,
you're given the world as a birthday present.

LEO BUSCAGLIA

Sleep, baby, sleep,
Our cottage vale is deep:
The little lamb is on the green,
With woolly fleece so soft and clean—
Sleep, baby, sleep.
Sleep, baby, sleep,
Down where the woodbines creep;
Be always like the lamb so mild,
A kind, and sweet, and gentle child.
Sleep, baby, sleep.

Mother Goose

A newborn baby is an extraordinary event; and I have
never seen two babies who looked exactly alike.

JAMES BALDWIN

Women have babies and men provide the support. If you don't like the way we're made you've got to take it up with God.

PHYLLIS SCHLAFLY

There is no finer investment for any community than putting milk into babies.

SIR WINSTON CHURCHILL

I love my wife more than anything in the world. But, boy, when she had our babies, it quadrupled. There's just something about the connection.

TIM MCGRAW

The reason teaching has to go on is that children are not born human; they are made so.

JACQUES BARZUN, American writer,
educator, and historian

A child who is to be successful is not reared exclusively on a bed of down.

GHANAIAN PROVERB

Don't forget that compared to a grownup person every baby is a genius. Think of the capacity to learn! The freshness, the temperament, the will of a baby a few months old!

MAY SARTON, poet and novelist

Every new baby is a blind desperate vote for survival: people who find themselves unable to register an effective political protest against extermination do so by a biological act.

LEWIS MUMFORD, American writer, architectural critic and urban planner

It is a pleasant thing to reflect upon, and furnishes a complete answer to those who contend for the gradual degeneration of the human species, that every baby born into the world is a finer one than the last.

CHARLES DICKENS, *Nicholas Nickleby*

I have always wanted to adopt a child and I am overjoyed that I have been blessed with a beautiful and healthy son. I'm completely enchanted and awe-struck.

CALISTA FLOCKHART, star of *Ally McBeal*

Mark the babe
Not long accustomed to this breathing world;
One that hath barely learned to shape a smile,
Though yet irrational of soul, to grasp
With tiny finger—to let fall a tear;
And, as the heavy cloud of sleep dissolves,
To stretch his limbs, bemocking, as might seem,
The outward functions of intelligent man.

WILLIAM WORDSWORTH

27

Tell me, what is half so sweet
As a baby's tiny feet?

EDGAR A. GUEST

If children grew up according to early indications,
we should have nothing but geniuses.

JOHANN WOLFGANG VON GOETHE

Except that right side up is best, there is not much to learn about holding a baby. There are one hundred and fifty-two distinctly different ways—and all are right!

HEYWOOD BROUN, American journalist and novelist

I once knew a chap who had a system of just hanging the baby on the clothes line to dry, and he was greatly admired by his fellow citizens for having discovered a wonderful innovation on changing a diaper.

DAMON RUNYON

When you have a baby, you set off an explosion in your marriage, and when the dust settles, your marriage is different from what it was. Not better, necessarily; not worse, necessarily; but different.

NORA EPHRON

Taking care of a newborn baby means devoting yourself, body and soul, twenty-four hours a day, seven days a week, to the welfare of someone whose response, in the way of positive reinforcement, is to throw up on you.

DAVE BARRY

Attachment to a baby is a long-term process, not a single, magical moment. The opportunity for bonding at birth may be compared to falling in love—staying in love takes longer and demands more work.

T. BERRY BRAZELTON, M.D.

29

The thing about having a baby is that thereafter you have it.

JEAN KERR, author of *Please Don't Eat the Daisies*

I knew I was pregnant before it was confirmed medically; you appeared to me in a dream, just as your brother, Nicolas did later…Those months you were inside me were a time of perfect happiness; I have never felt so closely accompanied.

ISABEL ALLENDE, novelist

…woman is frequently praised as the more "creative" sex. She does not need to make poems, it is argued; she has no drive to make poems, because she is privileged to make babies.

CYNTHIA OZICK

Despite compelling evidence that she will be working at 35, by choice or necessity, today's 21-year-old woman has difficulty looking beyond the ceremonies of her marriage and her babies' christenings.

MARILYN BENDER in *The New York Times*

You know, once you give birth, once you have kids, you realize what's important in life, and you realize it's really not difficult to be a good person. And so when people aren't good around me, I tend to move away from that. There are so many good people in the world, and you want to surround your children with that. I gave birth at home both times—natural—with a midwife, in water...with nothing.

PAMELA ANDERSON

Babies should enjoy the freedom to vocalize, whether it be in church, a public meeting place, during a movie, or after hours when the lights are out. They have not yet learned that joy and laughter have to last a lifetime and must be conserved.

ERMA BOMBECK

Without question, this is the
greatest thing I've done in my life.

JOHNNY DEPP on becoming a father

I don't dislike babies, though I think very young ones
rather disgusting.

QUEEN VICTORIA

Babies and gin and church
And women and Sunday
All mixed with dimes and
Dollars and clean spittoons
And house rent to pay.

LANGSTON HUGHES

Every mother believes she has the most beautiful baby, and every mother has a beautiful baby. That moment contains the essence of why I take photographs of babies. I believe every child is lovely, full of opportunity and promise.

ANNE GEDDES

I find that the most successful approach to the subject of babies is to discuss them as though they were hams; the firmness of the flesh, the pinkness of the flesh, the even distribution of fat, the sweetness and tenderness of the whole, and the placing of bone are the things to praise.

ROBERTSON DAVIES, *The Diary of Samuel Marchbanks*

Here we have a baby. It is composed
of a bald head and a pair of lungs.

EUGENE FIELD, Nineteenth
Century American poet

33

Precious and priceless,
So lovable, too—
The world's sweetest miracle,
Baby, is you.

HELEN STEINER RICE

I remember leaving the hospital—thinking, "Wait, are
they going to let me just walk off with him? I don't know
beans about babies! I don't have a license to do this."
We're just amateurs.

ANN TYLER

If you bungle raising your children, I don't think
whatever else you do well matters very much.

JACQUELINE KENNEDY ONASSIS

If one but realized it, with the onset of the first pangs of birth pains one begins to say farewell to one's baby. For no sooner has it entered the world when others begin to demand their share.

PRINCESS GRACE OF MONACO

And a woman who held a babe against her bosom said,
Speak to us of Children.
And he said:
Your children are not your children
They are the sons and daughters of Life's longing for itself
They come through you but not from you,
And though they are with you, yet they belong not to you.

KAHLIL GIBRAN, *The Prophet*

Parents are the bones on which children cut their teeth.

PETER USTINOV

✧✧✧✧✧

When Dad can't get the diaper on straight, we laugh at
him as though he were trying to walk around in high-heel
shoes. Do we ever assist him by pointing out that all you
have to do is lay out the diaper like a baseball diamond,
put the kid's butt on the pitcher's mound, bring home
plate up, then fasten the tapes at first and third base?

MICHAEL K. MEYERHOFF, "Of Baseball and Babies"

Raising kids is part joy
and part guerilla warfare.

ED ASNER

Nothing grows in our garden, only washing. And babies.

DYLAN THOMAS, *Under Milk Wood*

When those kids all go off to school you will be able to get a job running any major corporation in America. You will be the best-organized manager in the United States.

PRESIDENT BILL CLINTON to Bobbi McCaughey
after the birth of the septuplets

It is not economical to go to bed early to
save the candles if the result is twins.

CHINESE PROVERB

Well designed, fully functional infant. Provides someone to live for as well as another mouth to feed. Produces cooing, gurgling and other adorable sounds. May cause similar behavior in nearby adults. Cries when hungry, sleepy or just because. Hand Wash with warm water and mild soap, then pat dry with soft cloth and talc. Internal mechanisms are self-cleaning...Two Genders: Male. Female. Five Colors: White. Black. Yellow. Red. Camouflage.

ALFRED GINGOLD, Humorist

If your baby is "beautiful and perfect, never cries or fusses, sleeps on schedule and burps on demand, an angel all the time"...You're the grandma.

TERESA BLOOMINGDALE, Columnist

Spoil your baby. During the first year give him
all the attention he wants, because this is when he
is learning to love and trust.

LEE SALK, M.D.

All parents believe their children can do the impossible.
They thought it the minute we were born, and no matter
how hard we've tried to prove them wrong, they all think
it about us now. And the really annoying thing is, they're
probably right.

CATHY GUISEWITE

A little curly-headed, good-for-nothing,
And mischief-making monkey from his birth.

LORD BYRON, *Don Juan* (Canto I)

Good resolutions are like babies crying in church.
They should be carried out immediately.

REVEREND CHARLES M. SHELDON,
author of *In His Steps* (1896)

Interviewer: What about family? Is that on your
               agenda—to get married and have kids?

Drew Carey: No, not right now. I'm always at work.
               I feel bad about all the time I leave my
               dogs alone.

There never was a child so lovely
but his mother was glad to get him asleep.

RALPH WALDO EMERSON

There is no prince or prelate
I envy—no, not one.
No evil can befall me—
By God, I have a son!

CHRISTOPHER MORLEY

Spirit enters flesh
And for all it's worth
Charges into earth
In birth after birth
Ever fresh and fresh.

ROBERT FROST

Of children as of procreation—the pleasure momentary,
the posture ridiculous, the expense damnable.

EVELYN WAUGH, author of *Brideshead Revisited*

41

Envy the kangaroo. The pouch setup is extraordinary; the baby crawls out of the womb when it is about two inches long, gets into the pouch, and proceeds to mature. I'd have a baby if it would develop in my handbag.

RITA RUDNER

I have a profound protection instinct for this little one [the baby]. I look at him now, and for the first time in my life, I have something that I would do as much as I possibly can to protect and preserve and nurture.

CATHERINE ZETA-JONES

Only mothers can think of the future—because they give birth to it in their children.

MAXIM GORKY, Russian playwright and novelist

Birth may be a matter of a moment, but it is a unique one.

FREDERICK LEBOYER, M.D., author
of *Birth Without Violence*

When the first baby laughed for the first time, the laugh broke into a thousand pieces and they all went skipping about, and that was the beginning of fairies.

J. M. BARRIE, *Peter Pan*

When I take photographs of babies, I am saying,
"Look! Look at this baby, how lovely it is. See the way it lies, its little hands, its tummy—it's a marvel!"
It's my only message. I'm very passionate about it.

ANNE GEDDES

Since people are going to be living longer and getting older, they'll just have to learn how to be babies longer.

ANDY WARHOL

If in a shimmering room the babies came,
Drawn close by dreams of fledgling wing,
It was because night nursed them in its fold.

WALLACE STEVENS, "Palace of the Babies"

It is no small thing that they, who
are so fresh from God, love us.

CHARLES DICKENS

BABE or BABY, n. A misshapen creature of no particular age, sex, or condition, chiefly remarkable for the violence of the sympathies and antipathies it excites in others, itself without sentiment or emotion.

AMBROSE BIERCE

✧ ✧ ✧ ✧ ✧

Everyone knows that by far the happiest and universally enjoyable age of man is the first. What is there about babies which makes us hug and kiss and fondle them, so that even an enemy would give them help at that age?

DESIDERIUS ERASMUS

✧ ✧ ✧ ✧ ✧

An ugly baby is a very nasty object, and the prettiest is frightful when undressed.

QUEEN VICTORIA

I like trying [to get pregnant].
I'm not so sure about childbirth.

LAUREN HOLLY

The baby whose cries are answered now will later be
the child confident enough to show his independence
and curiosity.

LEE SALK, M.D.

46

Before you were conceived
    I wanted you
Before you were born
    I loved you
Before you were here an hour
    I would die for you
This is the miracle of life.

MAUREEN HAWKINS, "THE MIRACLE"

The watchful mother tarries nigh, though
sleep has closed her infant's eyes.

JOHN KEBLE, priest and poet

Let her have laughter with her little one;
    Teach her the endless, tuneless songs to sing,
Grant her her right to whisper to her son
    The foolish names one dare not call a king.

DOROTHY PARKER, "Prayer for a New Mother"

A bit of talcum
Is always walcum.

OGDEN NASH, "Ode to a Baby"

What good mothers and fathers instinctively feel like
doing for their babies is usually best after all.

BENJAMIN SPOCK, M.D. in *Life*

We can't form our children on our own concepts; we
must take them and love them as God gives them to us.

JOHANN WOLFGANG VON GOETHE

Give me the children until they are seven
and anyone may have them afterwards.

ST. FRANCIS XAVIER

Parents have become so convinced that educators
know what is best for their children that they forget
that they themselves are really the experts.

MARIAN WRIGHT EDELMAN, Staff Attorney for NAACP
and Founder of Children's Defense Fund (CDF)

Our birth is but a sleep and a forgetting;
The soul that rises with us, our life's star,
Hath had elsewhere its setting,
And cometh from afar;
Not in entire forgetfulness,
And not in utter nakedness,
But trailing clouds of glory do we come from
God, who is our home.

WILLIAM WORDSWORTH

The difference between writing a book and being on television is the difference between conceiving a child and having a baby made in a test tube.

NORMAN MAILER

Families with babies and families without babies are sorry for each other.

EDGAR WATSON HOWE, Nineteenth Century American editor, novelist, and essayist

Anyone who uses the phrase "easy as taking candy from a baby" has never tried taking candy from a baby.

ANONYMOUS

Do infants enjoy infancy as much as adults enjoy adultery?

GEORGE CARLIN

In automobile terms, the child supplies the power but the
parents have to do the steering.

Benjamin Spock, M.D.

The best babysitters, of course, are the baby's grandparents.
You feel completely comfortable entrusting your baby to
them for long periods, which is why most grandparents
flee to Florida at the earliest opportunity.

Dave Barry

Once you bring life into this world, you must protect it.
We must protect it by changing the world.

Elie Weisel

There is nothing in human nature more resonant with charges than the flow of energy between two biologically alike bodies, one of which has lain in amniotic bliss inside the other, one of which has labored to give birth to the other.

ADRIENNE RICH, American poet

My obstetrician was so dumb that when I gave birth
he forgot to cut the cord.
For a year that kid followed me everywhere.
It was like having a dog on a leash.

JOAN RIVERS

I've never been one for changing what is real in order to make my career buzz. My career comes second. There are some actors who do back-to-back jobs and are anxious when others are in the limelight. That's not me.

KATE WINSLET on taking maternity leave

If there's a camera there, it might stop me from saying, "I'm giving up, give me an epidural." It might make me tougher.

MAURA WEST, star of *As The World Turns*

Perhaps we share stories in much the same spirit that explorers share maps, hoping to speed each others journey, but knowing the journey we make will be our own.

GLORIA STEINEM on motherhood

And so you think a baby is a thing of beauty and a joy forever? Well, the idea is pleasing but not original; every cow thinks the same of its own calf.

MARK TWAIN

There is an amazed curiosity in every young mother. It is strangely miraculous to see and to hold a living being formed within oneself and issued forth from oneself.

SIMONE DE BEAUVOIR

Moving between the legs of tables and of chairs,
Rising or falling, grasping at kisses and toys,
Advancing boldly, sudden to take alarm,
Retreating to the corner of arm and knee,
Eager to be reassured, taking pleasure
In the fragrant brilliance of the Christmas tree…

T.S. ELIOT

What is a child, monsieur, but the image of two beings, the fruit of two sentiments spontaneously blended?

HONORÉ DE BALZAC

Out of the mouths of babes and sucklings
hast thou ordained strength.

PSALMS 8:2

Where did you come from, Baby dear?
Out of the everywhere into the here.
Where did you get your eyes so blue?
Out of the sky as I came through.

GEORGE MACDONALD, *At the*
Back of the North Wind

When we are born we cry that we are come…
to this great stage of fools.

WILLIAM SHAKESPEARE

55

Woman is the artist of the imagination and the child in the womb is the canvas whereon she painteth her pictures.

PARACELSUS, Fifteenth Century physician

You are entirely engrossed in your own body and the life it holds. It is as if you were in the grip of a powerful force; as if a wave had lifted you above and beyond everyone else. In this way there is always a part of a pregnant woman that is unreachable and is reserved for the future.

SOPHIA LOREN

I didn't know how babies were made until I was pregnant with my fourth child.

LORETTA LYNN

The woman about to become a mother, or with her newborn infant upon her bosom, should be the object of trembling care and sympathy wherever she bears her tender burden or stretches her aching limbs....God forbid that any member of the profession to which she trusts her life, doubly precious at that eventful period, should hazard it negligently, unadvisedly or selfishly.

OLIVER WENDELL HOLMES

Your clear eye
Is the one absolutely beautiful thing
I want to fill it
With colors and ducks
The zoo of the new

SYLVIA PLATH

The only time a woman really succeeds in
changing a man is when he's a baby.

NATALIE WOOD

My mother groan'd, my father wept;
Into the dangerous world I leapt,
Helpless, naked, piping loud,
Like a fiend hid in a cloud.

WILLIAM BLAKE

When a baby looks into a caregiver's face—that person's, that mother's, that father's—it's the map of that child's world. And if those maps are always changing, that world can become very frightening.

MR. [FRED] ROGERS

The moment a child is born,
The mother is also born.
She never existed before.
The woman existed, but the mother, never.
A mother is something absolutely new.

OSHO (FORMERLY BHAGWAN SHREE RAJNEESH)

Most experts agree that the roots of joy, fear, and anger take hold at a very young age. Right from birth, babies are social beings, interested in interacting with other people. Feelings are their first language. As babies get older and learn more about the world around them, their capacity to feel emotions grows with their ability to express them.

JENNY FRIEDMAN, PH.D. in *American Baby*

Small children disturb your sleep, big children your life.

YIDDISH PROVERB

Don't forget that compared to a grownup person every baby is a genius. Think of the capacity to learn! The freshness, the temperament, the will of a baby a few months old!

MAY SARTON, American poet and novelist

If a woman has to choose between catching a fly ball and saving an infant's life, she will choose to save the infant's life without even considering if there are men on base.

DAVE BARRY

My day-old son is plenty scrawny,
His mouth is wide with screams, or yawny,
His ears seem larger than he's needing.
His nose is flat, his chin receding,
His skin is very, very red,
He has no hair upon his head,
And yet I'm proud as proud can be
To hear you say he looks like me.

RICHARD ARMOUR

The family is one of nature's masterpieces.

GEORGE SANTAYANA

War will never cease until babies begin to come into the world with larger cerebrums and smaller adrenal glands.

H.L. MENCKEN

You have to love your children unselfishly.
That's hard. But it's the only way.

BARBARA BUSH

Somewhere on this globe, every ten seconds, there is a woman giving birth to a child. She must be found and stopped.

SAM LEVENSON, American humorist

Babies are such a nice way to start people.

DON HEROLD, American cartoonist and humorist

A mother learns a whole new language—the language of love and the language of baby talk. Although no one else understands her baby, the mother knows exactly what he is saying.

RACHEL KELLER, journalist

We are intellectually still babies; this is perhaps why a baby's facial expression so strangely suggests the professional philosopher.

GEORGE BERNARD SHAW

When I approach a child, he inspires in me two sentiments: tenderness for what he is and a respect for what he may become.

LOUIS PASTEUR

The first cry of a newborn baby in Chicago or Zamboango, in Amsterdam or Rangoon, has the same pitch and key, each saying "I am! I have come through! I belong!"

CARL SANDBURG

Children make you want to start life over.

MUHAMMAD ALI

Even just on a selfish level…[kids] enrich you. But it's the hardest thing in the world, especially for someone who is independent.

LISA KUDROW, Star of *Friends*

We must learn the loving of a first child step by step, as we learn to sustain love in marriage. The loving of a first baby is like an acquired gift, or skill. The second child, I imagine, comes into that love ready-made.

FRANCES KARLEN SANTAMARIA

How could I have forgotten that each time, each birth is not only a first for the baby but a renewal for all of us who will love and cherish her?

LOIS WYSE, *Grandchildren are so much fun,*
I should have had them first

Making the decision to have a child—it's momentous. It is to decide forever to have your heart go walking around outside your body.

ELIZABETH STONE